IN THE KNEES OF THE GODS

In the Greeke alwayes this phrase is used,
not in the hands, but ἐν γούνασι κεῖται,
in the knees of the gods lies our helps . . .

—George Chapman

IN THE KNEES OF THE GODS

POEMS

TRISH REEVES

BkMk Press
University of Missouri-Kansas City

BkMk Press
University of Missouri-Kansas City
5101 Rockhill Road
Kansas City, Missouri 64110
(816) 235-2558 (voice)
(816) 235-2611 (fax)
bkmk@umkc.edu
http://www.umkc.edu/bkmk/

Financial assistance for this project has been made possible
by the Missouri Arts Council, a state agency.

Book design by Roxanne Marie Witt
Cover art by James Thomas Stevens

Printing by McNaughton & Gunn

Library of Congress Cataloguing-in-Publication Data

Reeves, Trish, 1947-
    In the knees of the gods : poems / Trish Reeves.
        p. cm.
    ISBN 1-886157-31-6
    1.   Women—Poetry. I. Title.

PS3568.E474 I5 2001
811'.54—dc21

                                            00-049845

10   9   8   7   6   5   4   3   2   1

For
Marilyn Anne Hutchinson

Acknowledgments

Some of the poems have been published in the following magazines, to whose editors grateful acknowledgment is made:

13th Moon, "Something Infinite"; *Any Key Review*, "Holy Faith," "Seascape"; *First Intensity*, "Duval Street," "Greene Street," "Simonton Street," "White Street Pier," "The Walk from the House at Crane Point," "The End of the Dock," "Tin Roof"; *Forum*, "Painting Light"; *Helicon Nine*, "Van Gogh Aims for Own Heart and Misses"; *Helicon Nine Hunger Relief Anthology: Spud Songs*, "Of Potatoes"; *Mid-American Review*, "The Beautiful Golden Bareback Rider"; *New Letters*, "Don't," "Entrance to the View," "January," "What Do I Have of You," "April," "Chronology," "From the Garden, St. Rémy," "My Friend and I Try To Out-Argue Our Notions About Einstein's Brain," "In Which I Elevate Myself to Sainthood," "Of the Night," "Picture at Impact"; *Passages North*, "The Elements"; *Phoenix Papers Anthology*, "Dark Chopin Tie"; *Potpourri*, "*Giornata*"; *Prairie Schooner*, "Twilight," "When the Farmers Come to Town," "I Started Subscribing," "Meditation"; *Review*, "Slow Gold."

I wish to thank Yaddo and the National Endowment for the Arts. Special thanks to Glenda McCrary, Michael Pritchett, Adele Sheehan and James Thomas Stevens. —T.R.

Contents

III

IV

I

Of the Night

What was it like in those caves
on the nights when the soul fled
so far from the animal
it inhabited that the artist, awakened,
crawled, pulling the last of the dry moss
from the pouch to touch it to the dark
but living sticks of the fire pit
and then, pelt-draped, huddled, in the shelter of that
    small light,
needing to see the reminders roaming
the walls, speaking out of fur and figure
and fortitude: Here's your life
right outside your door, herds
of it, and here is your hand outlined
in charcoal.   All that must happen
is for you, again, tomorrow,
to fetch your sharpened stick,
leave the warmth
of this room and all that civilizes and centers
you—to creep across the frozen earth
long enough to win your life back
in bites, mouthfuls and so finally
pull the soul back from the crevice
of the cave, feel the soul slip into your fingers
as you grab a long black ember
for one more sweep across the wall, the message:
This is the life I have taken
today to sustain this gesture
that must speak for me

of how I endure, how hard the hunt
when there is no one here at my return,
and how great my love, nevertheless,
for the clear and studied sight of this hand
steady upon the wall.

For those who have so pushed the darkness away
when I first awakened, I am grateful;
for all they cannot do,
I awaken a second time and weep.

Of the Dawn

I wish you were here with me
to see the first light drifting
down from Moon Mountain
as I reach for you
to describe with my mouth
the way the early morning shadows feel
as they fall in blues and lavenders, my tongue
on your breast, then your mouth again; the sounds
from the arroyos now of domestic
creatures, leashed,
where, in the last hours of night,
coyotes, fur brushed
by the same strict sand and sage, laughed
with us through the skin-splitting
flashes streaking the sky,
instructing us in the second:
She is here, seek her gently with your teeth.

In Which I Elevate Myself to Sainthood

You must take the will for the deed.
                    —Jonathan Swift

As if warm milk would put me to sleep
I pour a whole pitcher full. Call it

a miracle, I say, as my eyelids close
and orbs beneath them lift from the land

of the healed and the never to be so;
simple levitation in accordance

with my wishes taking me to table
after small gilded table of seated

saints: Joan, Teresa, Kateri, and
Bernadette of the undiminished

passions; patting the cushions beside them,

whispering of misunderstandings,
intimacies they must share

only with me, one more curl of fire
and shadow performing an impossible feat.

En Face

The way a woman
carries silence in her womb
until the child touches air—
that's how I went looking for you,
your naked touch,
your form vaguely specific.

When I found you
and you threw your shawl about us,
those who looked from windows,
even those who stared for hours,
could set no example.

Picture at Impact

It is 1855 and
two women are embracing—
their arms around each other's
bare shoulders. If you haven't seen
French daguerreotypes, I will acquaint you.
One of these French girls
looks like me—caught
young and angry in the command
to hold still with another—while wanting
to move with her body, her breathing
no matter the world be watching
for the slightest stir
or beat of the heart. Only my wish
to present us immoveable in our embrace
overcomes my desire
to blur our bodies with motion.
So we appear serene
as one can be staring into another's eye.
Our photographer behind the camera—
warm in his frock coat
and collar—Stay still as death,
he whispers.
Unflinching, I hold her tighter.

Love and Art

Does he not fear sleeping and dreaming of her?
          —Kakimoto no Hitomaro

The hope of seeing her still haunts me.
          —Ariwara no Narihira

Because I can't sleep
because of you
I prop on pillows on this near-empty bed
and use the book to write on—
having found so little in the oversized
pages of *Erotic Art of Japan.*
Only one picture of two women
who wanted each other enough
to find themselves in a world of women
with men. The two women together
are so interwoven in their print
I had to close the book
unable to tell them apart.

I wanted to make sense of that picture.
All day, beginning when I left you,
after we had sat so close together,
you speaking of your heart,
me wanting to throw myself at your knees,
all day I've tried separating women from each other.
I cannot.
And I cannot sleep.

Something Infinite

Tonight I want to go to one of those parties
where women dance with each other,
because that dance
seems to me the closest way
to talk about time
and mean something infinite
beyond my two children
sleeping in this house where their father
is sleeping, while I stay at my desk
wishing I could ask for no more,
but wanting only a woman,
no time,
just that woman   tonight
tomorrow
and days after
so numerous as to seem unnumbered.

Painting Light

*. . . but at this time of year the sun sets so fast
that I can't follow it . . .*
                        — Claude Monet

I've gone as far as to close my eyes
to focus. Yes, of course I still see
his shoulders and trousers
and her figure wearing the straw hat
become a pile of clothes topped by straw
with strokes of orange flecking the yellow.
I'm concentrating on haystacks right now—
garden dresses afire. Afire!

I have to stop myself, no more than thirty minutes
at the meadow—then next day
I go back and throw my palette
to the stubble—everything is changed
though the weather and hour are identical.
Only remembering the flush on the girl's
arm makes me pick up the palette.

Can you see the sun from your window?
Two days ago it woke me. Intense
as August. Yet when I raised to my elbow
and looked over my shoulder it had thinned.
Have you ever been awakened by
that much, that little light?

I never had. I now know it was not the light
that awakened me, but the dream.

Old Photograph

But haven't we been there, another
couple, the woods, one woman's hand
close to the bit, the horse's coat shiny, ribs
exposed under the sheen as you, in your white
swath of dress, hold what I hesitate to call
a whip, so delicate, so suspended in the invisible,
and so far from dropping through
those many molecules
it must move
to stir the mount and every breath
of air around us.

The Beautiful Golden Bareback Rider

Take out your health books, please,
and turn to the page
of the drawing of the beautiful
lady standing on tiptoes
on the back of the horse. This is a lesson:
Never paint yourself gold
without leaving
a small spot, perhaps under your arms—
for the skin to breathe through. You see this woman
in the drawing, so young, so beautiful, so near death
the tragedy leaves every one of us
with never another thought
of painting ourselves gold,
never another thought that we might so change
ourselves without the greatest risk—
for it would be so like us
to forget to leave that place
where the truth breathes through.

II

Chronology

"Goes out into the field
and shoots himself."
Well wouldn't you know
this is the guy we adore.
The wheat wild with him,
the crows crazed and we
so undecided
about life ourselves
that the least mention
of Arles and
self-portraits put on *impasto*
has us thumbing through
our pasts for the date
he entered them with his sorrow
as vividly as a death in the family
that links us to our
fate like the calendar
on which numbers are unnecessary.

When the Farmers Come to Town

I will not go to the market today
where the thick-handed man sells dirty radishes,
the plucked chickens lie on pink ice
and if it were not for the rich wool sweaters
on Saturday outings
everyone there would be poor,
shopping out of necessity
at the back of the pickup beds.

I must have gotten into that truck
from my grandfather's side.
Crawled through the tobacco air
asking him to roll down my window, please.
Too young to see over the dash
to understand where we were going
even when we were there.

Inside the old house the AA rented
I was an oddity.
Fistfuls of men in every room
and one little girl
they lifted up to sit on the wall
in back, on good days.

Sometimes the men were so worried
about the sick people upstairs
I would just sit quietly,
one in the endless rows of empty chairs
in the dusky front room,
watching the vacant stairwell
for my grandfather

to come down from upstairs.
I did not belong there,
I did not belong in that truck,
I didn't belong in the farm house it left from
every Saturday
and today, when my friend I do not belong with
calls me, I think about pulling on a sweater
pretending I can afford this time away from myself
at the market where I will buy nothing.

The Elements

There is a street in Kansas
where men stand with grain
in their hands, waiting.
When the wind whips down the street
they throw the grain with an upward arc
so that it falls downward
like snow
with the fast force of wind behind it.
The men stand with empty hands,
the grain stinging their faces.
They say, This is what life does to me
every day.

Crying Wolf

The first cautionary tale
I remember. Maybe I've always done it—
that must have been the reason my mother told me:
a beloved boy, a ragged wolf—ice in her eyes
as she read—or maybe
it was the first bad idea
I picked up from literature,
at the time thinking I'd
know when to quit:
one story before
they sensed that all I wanted
was a voice in the fear
everywhere around me.

Twilight

If I took the small brass cricket box outside
at this very moment
would I be able to fill it with luck.
Would I be able to believe
the reasons my husband spends two nights away
and one night here,
that there is health
in my children's adult-like grasp
of the situation,
naturalness in my inability to cry.

Would I find the sounds
of small creatures
place a spell on all of this sadness
and we would see out,
my children and I and my absent husband,
would see out of this house
as if it were a gold box cut with intention
to reveal to us a world so dazzling
it could only be taken in pieces
and each piece would delight us
in an interwoven way:
My son would see red-suited soldiers,
my daughter would see the soldiers
never fire a shot,
my husband and I would see no soldiers.
And all of our tears would be of joy,
the joy that comes
from moving from one point of view to another,
from really seeing the world

as the one you love just saw it.
The joy of saying, Look!
and, I see!

Does it do any good to love every one of us
who moves in and out of this house.
Of course.
Who can stop.
Who can stop to go outside
to fill a box with crickets.

Oh if there could be a God,
if luck could sing from every word on this page.

Last Night

Our bodies were so smooth against each other
fit so well
it was as if we were young again
not 40 and 45
but 20, 25.
Our young selves—
not me asking silently,
Is this the last time?
Not you unable to say, finally unable to say,
We will always have this.

I try not to tell you, now, that I love you.
But last night
the words escaped like tears
unwanted by either of us,
an embarrassment accompanying my unspoken,
How can you be fucking us both,
an embarrassment accompanying you
flaunting an unspoken love.

January

The month after you left
for good, I pulled both of my desks
into the bedroom, and the bookshelves,
though there was no room,
I could no longer have my books so far away,
so I lined the hall with them.
Really not too narrow now in the hallway,
but warm, I told the children, and,
Help yourselves, I told the children.
These books are for all of us—
no longer mine to stash
in a far part of the house,
but here, for the three of us
to turn to on our way through the dark hall.
Every poet you see
by our night light
is here, living in our house
to remind you
that when you chill
without the touch of your father
pull every warm word
you can find
around you.

Dark Chopin Tie

I'm sitting on the couch listening
when my daughter walks in.
She asks me if I'm listening to Mozart,
she tells me the mother across the street is listening
to Mozart. I'm listening to Chopin.
I hold up the plastic CD case
to show my daughter the picture. Chopin, I say.
I know little
about this kind of music but that to listen to it
helps. And then I'm startled, I see the dark brown eyes
of Chopin, the erratic cut of hair.
I stop myself from saying:
He looks like your father,
doesn't he look like the man I divorced today,
the man I was married to at 11 am,
the man I divorced at 41,
the man who was not there for his no-fault divorce
in Court 13 on March 13th.
The divorce that was followed by
three other women in line
for no-faults before noon.
Mozart, Chopin
the three women behind me in Court 13,
I trust them: the women would say
my husband was actually there this morning,
they had sensed him in his white collar
and dark Chopin tie
just as I would have to say
I sensed their husbands
though it was their absence
that explained the women's lives to me
like music.

Don't

. . . experience has been the mistress of those who wrote well.
—Leonardo da Vinci

Don't you know all the paintings are still lifes—
the river not so much running
as remaining,
the woman at the well
able to keep the lambs beside her
with her calm.
Even the stomping of hooves rests
upon shields and graves.
Talk as much as you like
about energy on a canvas,
pace before it to keep blood in your body
but never tell me I have what I want
when I tell you
John Keats keeps me alive.
Touch me, and I'll treat you badly.

April

It was something we did in our thirties,
mounting up at the outskirts
of town after several drinks, then
riding the horses
through the birthing cries
of the coyotes, badgers; hooves smashing
through morels, death angels; bobcats
mating all along our way
into the downtown, past the tall
Episcopalian and Presbyterian
spires, up the steps on horseback, hooves splintering
the risers into our private club, the one exclusive
club in town, to proclaim
not a cultural awakening,
sword dangling, but how very drunk
we could get in that small river town,
having just passed
the smell of the spawning season
in the month when the bees divide their colonies,
the planting moon a month away,
nine more foolish months
from what we, so stepped out
of our lives,
forecast as forever on the horizon.

Giornata

I'll give anyone, today, wings—
the woman leading the small boy
away, the servant girl
flying down the stairs, even golden
feathers to lift the body of the lamb.
Good people, good animals, and
if the grass and trees
become too familiar, I'll
attach wings to their graceful stalks.

Have you seen water flying?
Ointment of luminous lime
and sand is water flying.

As beginning again
in this world every morning
is like flying into this wall.
Today I will not embrace the wall
unprotected.

Van Gogh Aims for Own Heart
and Misses

I say to her, There's the van Gogh,
the one painting of his
this museum owns
because the painter is so great
that even out here in Kansas
we can walk right up to the edge
of that olive grove,
we can see the artist standing outside
the grasping blue trees
and know he'd been down the paths
he painted in blue.

I say to her, There's the Turner.
I find myself unable to leave the shore
of Hastings, back and forth
from the door of the gallery
to the painting again; at last
obeying her hurry I speak words
as some way to bear
the leaving. I say, Look at that light,
look at that light become water.

When I go home I have no copy
of the shore at Hastings, only
a patch of clearness in my mind.
And the postcard of the Oise
at Auvers, boats of color, prospect:

one woman already seated in the green boat,
another about to step into the blue.

The woman already seated could be my mother.
Each boat, finally, could carry a heart
that refused to be reached.

My Friend and I Try to Out-Argue Our Notions About Einstein's Brain

For Glenda

Yes, it has been dissected.

No, not enough has been done. Not enough,
how could I say such a thing?

Enough to know it's different.

Yes, but the slides could say more, and
that's what those other scientists want, those
slides and bottles and other ways
the most private part of the man is stored,
removed from behind the brow and voice
that said, Yes, this is private; No, it's not.
And all the people said, He's so smart he knows
not to use the weapon he's bright enough to build,
he advised against it. We say, He's so smart
only a handful understand what he thought,
just as we might advise against something about his brain
but can't quite put it in words,
yet, enough has been done; it is different,
perhaps even certain he's no longer in Princeton,
maybe never dwelling on the fact that by some mistake
a researcher turned doctor ended up with his brain
and took it with him to dusty Weston, Missouri, where
the demands on the small-town practitioner keep him
from finding time to study what he can't let go of,
     the contents
of a couple of cardboard boxes the cleaning woman
     must move to
do her work in the cinder-block clinic I drove by

years ago to try to conceptualize
that 30 miles from where I lay my head to pillow
in Prairie Village, Kansas, 30 miles away
our famous and favorite A. Einstein
travels through eternity, at least his most remarked upon
aspect travels through eternity without the assistance of
    stranger
or friend or aging body to take him home.

The Many Mornings of Infinity

Would you please tell me
what it's like to be dead?

Certainly, first you wake up
and you're alive.

Why is this the kind of answer
I would expect from you?

Because you ask believing
that you can't know,

you who've already forgotten
what it was like this morning to awaken

you who did not notice.

III

Sublime Exhibition!
Heaven-Borne Conjuror

The only amateurs are the people who paint badly.
        —Édouard Manet

As in making love without saying,
I love you.

To slip inside the hour glass
is the trick.
No need to separate the sea
and stack one side upon the other
like a tidy prophet
or magniloquent illusionist,
but simply to say, your body become
sand: Time could never contain me
        until I was pulled from the sea
        and brought together
        to slip through the narrows of the present
        as expansive as if I were
        the past or the future. Aware,
        unaware. Astonishing, sublime exhibition.

Duval Street

Immodest as a vertebrate,
and still possessing hind limbs

give me something
orange or blue or pink
to wrestle,
              flesh to unfold like ribs
of a parasol.

Humid morning, please
promise me a lover to straddle
this tropical night, parrots screeching
from freedom,
              orchid body
through my skin; oh

              small island, outlandish love.

Greene Street

Sit before me, please.

Bull's eye; the louvered doors are open
floor to ceiling, the oysters
served, shimmer of silver seats
each animal, splash of pepper from the slender
bottle; I swallow you, two days
hence, I'll drive again this bridge,
long arch, fragile linkage
like the scent of gardenia,
to the white marl island.

On your knees now;
that's the way
I mount this memory.

Simonton Street

The dolphin's cup yields
sheets and sheets of navy blue sky—
I feel your fingers around my wrists; your mouth,
capable of anything I want, whispers,
Show me your losses.

Salvor, the reason I love you:
there is nothing I am not
to show you of the sea.

White Street Pier

When I met you; no
that's not the truth of it, but if I had met you
at the end of White Street Pier, two bathers—
though no one bathes from that height
where there is no gentle letting down
into the sea, where there is no nakedness,
but of concrete and the ocean water
slow and full
with brown debris of fronds and grass and the wind
of sand—
but you weren't coming to meet me,
to be the one figure approaching as I turned
at the end of the walk, surprise swept
above the southern sea.
                              If you had shown up
that late afternoon, I would say,
Life appeared to me at last
in the body of a woman; the sea, surrounded by us,
surrendered; yes, life
is that succulent
and swift.

The way it is, I don't know how long
I've been on this pier.

Seascape

But all I want is you—

float me some love
if you can,
I could be there by eight—

I want night with you;
I want it the way a reef claims a ship,
the way you took me down

what I know is your imagery
outweighs my soul
and only your mouth
can take the salt from the sea
and place it on my tongue again.

The Walk from the House at Crane Point

As if I could have lived with you
in that house, awakened, your body
still and formed to mine like a hammock
just before I reached for you with my mouth, tongue
salt-tolerant as the darling plum.
                              As if someone
wouldn't have thought us immoral—and that
not the problem, not the point
at the moment when we passed
the army jeep pulled to the edge of the ocean,
empty seats, empty lookout
shaded by thatch palms—
just past the cottage made by man and wife,
thick marl walls, deep silled in its banyan
and shaving brush setting.

Ask me the new fashion, the same desire
in which I would have lived
in the oldest house on the island
with you.

The End of the Dock

I've checked around
and no one's told me, *Shouldn't be so hard*—
the longed for, certainly sought
branch, sea blossom
of you beside me
stepping down the soft dock
to the end where the sea
surrounds us, mated by salt,
ocean our socket
for what moves within.

The roosters call from shore,
the fishermen turn their eyes from us
into the light wind
so as not to see
what they know
of loss.

Tin Roof

It's still Key West
I wake to in the night,
the reef irreparably cut, rubble
of stars scattered on stones
washed and dried,
then washed and dried again
as if a cleansing, as if a cleansing
of my face, breast, body
of you
were possible, or the weather could be kept
from the roof,
                    the weather and your body
no longer powering the night,
no longer singing me awake and then to sleep again.

IV

Of Potatoes

We didn't plan our lives this way—
to be taken by the plate
of potatoes, glass of beer,
the bed that came after
always asking for us
to give to love
as if it were a charity
that would cost us no more,
once we threw ourselves like a coin
into the great world of need
and declared ourselves
more blessed.

We, the bitten and bounced back,
casting the same gold coin, still
wanting the blessing,
still wanting to have a bit more
than the poor.

I Started Subscribing

to the *Christian Science Monitor*
as a way to get more politics
into my poetry. The first night of the subscription
I dreamed of execution—
mine. I couldn't remember the trial or
offense but focused on the envelope
in my hands
that held the papers I called
"my traveling papers," my dry wit showing I was well-
adjusted, at last, to life,
the getting-out part, at least. The third time I
tried the "traveling papers" humor,
no longer with my friends, but other
women prisoners on a bus, all of us
headed for our own deaths, one woman
began to cry; I vaguely
remembered her from my first-grade class,
vaguely remembered she'd overcome being
the poor girl by becoming an M.D. (studies
say doctors fear death the most). I wondered
what she'd done to be on this bus—something
botched? I felt bad
when I saw I'd made her cry; realized the same
old self-interest of the love poem
still ran through me. And this, of course,
frightened me a bit, enough
to make me see the stretcher and straps, enough
to cause me to open my envelope.
And what luck for me
that I was finally taking an interest in the business of life—

for the envelope held four photographs,
various head views, full frontal, profile, etc.,
of the doomed woman sitting on the stand,
so no mistakes
would be made in the death chamber,
I supposed. The woman on the stand,
though she looked a bit like me,
was not, clearly was
not, because I do not own
a brooch like the one she wore at her neck.
At this realization, I was becoming more joyful
than all the jokes in the world could make me.
Looking further into the envelope, at the account
of my crime, I knew all I needed
was a phone call—this was
a mistake, certainly I'd committed
no crime of heterosexual passion—
all of my lovers for the last eight years
had been women—
Stop this bus! I said,
I'm not as guilty as we thought—
I'm not the woman of the photos—
Not yet, said the driver, and the bus kept rolling
as he told all the women
to check their envelopes.
There's been a mix up, he said.

Embrace

The way she drove us into the stone wall,
I thought I could probably do as well,
whether the goal was
to hit the wall
or to not hit the wall.

So most of my life,
I have been homesick
for the wall, my hands
all over the steering wheel
as if it were the body of a woman
I desired, first one way, then another
until I became the object
of her despair
and she for me,
the wheel wrenched from my hands
at the moment my forehead
collapsed into the column of sky.

Come Hear

I don't want you, Des.
I don't want you now—
you didn't come when I wanted you
and now I don't want you.
Des is two; this deep in the barn
his blond hair is the source of light
as he stands to the side
of the Arabian, Des, with fingers in mouth
doesn't seem to know where to go. His mother
pulls the saddle off
and almost smiles
at Des's father's words.
I don't want you Des.
Des is growing into me.
I keep looking at Des's father,
keep thinking he will apologize,
Apologize, say you'll never say that again.
I look at Des,
the dust covering our boots
as we pace in place.

Entrance to the View

First the view is dark, right,
that's all we remember, or don't remember
but must believe to be so
unless we believe in light—
not the notation of light
but the goldness of the waves,
gold blur in the eyes
of the sailor, and golden
rocks on the shore, rocks so bright
that if you saw one you would never
remember any other
way of remembering the darkness
of the sea, darkness behind the
tongue, dust on the body
of the earth as she holds your coat.

Holy Faith

In the bar under the cottonwoods
that night, you, in your torn black jeans,
could have called me *Timberline*
and I would have
trailed you through the arroyos
in the dark
to the top of the mountain
where I walk into my name,
the dog star nipping
at the moon, *santos* and sand
in the air, our fingers
like petroglyphs
reaching off the surface of stone.

To You

Where I'd like to be
with you
is midway through a
Cavafy poem; blue
sounds breaking around the
island, white
outline of window
no longer noticed
by the two lovers, two women
in place of Cavafy's young men,
two women so sure
of the source of light
and the other
that there is more
to the slow kiss
than a poet can place
on the page,
more of summer than
sculptor or open shutter can reveal,
more to the encounter
than conclusion.

From the Garden, St. Rémy

We take death to go to a star.
                    —Vincent van Gogh

If we share a blueness of eye, a violet-blue of irises,
they are not the same sharp blue—
though equally vivid—anymore
than the stars equal one another in color
as they burn their presence into the sky
long enough to please generations
but little longer than a blossoming, though it takes a
    clear eye
to discern the difference between definition
and diminishment
while standing in a garden of blue eyes
looking up; the horses impatient at the gate,
each ready to carry us
to what we suppose
the same, but different, death.

Slow Gold

Would you choose to live
if it were before
the discovery of fire,
          and your helpmeet
had broken a leg
and arm and when
they didn't mend
and the infection didn't clear
with the cobwebs
          and there was no pyre
for either of you,
no way to light the sticks
to take away the stench,
no light for later
that night of the day
when even the seer
born to address this death
was unable to say,
Ashes to ashes.

Meditation

Imperceptibly they [objects] extend beyond themselves
through intimate reflections, as we do by looks and words . . .
                    —Paul Cézanne

As during that whole month of rain and the two of us
locked in the beauty
of the other,
never needing to say, Help me with her, God;
but having breast and breath at command
and the color and the grammar of it
and the calm gaze of the eye
before passion—
before the redefining fatigue
of concentration and caress.

And for this rain and life
I have given myself—entry
delivering me
to the moment, the mutual possession of the apple
    and Eve,
she who pierces and is so taken.

Notes

Giornata (page 26)
"Giornata" is the term for the amount of fresco painting executed in one day.

Slow Gold (page 52)
The phrase "Slow Gold" is from line 5 of poem "406" by Emily Dickinson.

About the Author

Trish Reeves, a graduate of the University of Missouri-Columbia School of Journalism and the Warren Wilson College MFA Program, was born and raised in Missouri. Her first book of poems, *Returning the Question,* received the Cleveland State University Poetry Center Prize. She has received fellowships for her poetry from the National Endowment for the Arts, Yaddo and the Kansas Arts Commission. Reeves currently lives in Kansas.